I0820061

The Brandy Milk Punch

The Brandy Milk Punch

SHARON KEATING &
CHRISTI KEATING SUMICH

LOUISIANA STATE UNIVERSITY PRESS
BATON ROUGE

Published by Louisiana State University Press
lsupress.org

Manufactured in the United States of America
First printing

Designer: Barbara Neely Bourgoyne
Typeface: Arno Pro
Printer and binder: Integrated Books International

Cover photograph courtesy Sam Gregory Anselmo.

Frontispiece courtesy AdobeStock/Brent Hofacker.
All photographs are by the authors unless otherwise credited.

Library of Congress Cataloging-in-Publication Data
Names: Keating, Sharon, author. | Sumich, Christi Keating, author.
Title: The brandy milk punch / Sharon Keating and Christi Keating Sumich.
Description: Baton Rouge : Louisiana State University Press, [2025] |
Includes bibliographical references.
Identifiers: LCCN 2024033326 | ISBN 978-0-8071-8353-3 (cloth)
Subjects: LCSH: Milk punches—History. | Brandy—Louisiana—
New Orleans—History. | LCGFT: Cookbooks.
Classification: LCC TX951.3.M55 K335 2025 | DDC
641.2/530976335—dc23/eng/20240910
LC record available at https://lccn.loc.gov/2024033326

To our families, for wholeheartedly supporting our mother-daughter writing venture. It's been too much fun, and we couldn't have done it without you!

CONTENTS

ACKNOWLEDGMENTS

Like many New Orleanians, we love a good cocktail, and we love discussing cocktails: where to get them, how to make them, and so on. So, writing a book about cocktails seemed like a perfect fit for us. However, writing an entire book about one cocktail was more than a little daunting. We soon realized that taking a deep dive into the history, ingredients, and culture of the brandy milk punch was a fascinating endeavor and one that we could not have completed without help. We would like to thank Jenny Keegan, our editor who guided us through the process, along with the rest of the Louisiana State University Press staff. Thank you to the staff of the Historic New Orleans Collection, in particular Robert Ticknor and Heather Green, for the generous use of their photographs in this book. To Chris Hannah, co-owner of Jewel of the South and mixologist extraordinaire, thank you for your patience in answering all our questions and for serving us one of the best brandy milk punches we have ever tasted. There would be no brandy milk punch book if not for the bars and restaurants who serve up the drink to locals and tourists alike all over the city of New Orleans. We thank them, especially those who so generously shared their recipes with us: the folks at Brennan's, Commander's Palace, Galatoire's, Bourbon House, Mr. B's, and Broussard's. Finally, we would like to thank our husbands: Wayne Keating, for serving once again as our photographer; and Leni Sumich, for cheerfully putting up with our shenanigans. We love you!

The Brandy Milk Punch

Brandy milk punch
[AdobeStock/Mayatnikstudio]

Introduction

ROLLING WITH THE PUNCH(ES)

> To get over the guilt of drinking, take your brandy in milk. This way, it becomes medicinal.
>
> —CATHERINE COOKSON

Picture this nostalgic New Orleans Christmas scene: the tree is sparkling with a rainbow of colorful bulbs made even more magical as the tinsel reflects the light in shimmering prisms. Bing Crosby is on the hi-fi crooning about a white Christmas, even though it's currently 82 degrees with 78 percent humidity outside. It's a vintage Christmas (like the home movies Clark Griswold watches in *Christ-*

mas Vacation), only NOLA style, with Maison Blanche boxes under the tree and K&B ice cream in the deep freeze for dessert. What adult beverage are you enjoying? Brandy milk punch, of course. The delicate hint of nutmeg makes each sip taste like the holidays. It has all the things you love about eggnog, only lighter and silkier (and, of course, without the egg).

Now the scene switches to a chilly February morning. It's been a long Carnival parade season, and the brisk weather and multi-krewe lineup call for some hair of the dog. As you lounge on your thrift-store loveseat, placed strategically on the neutral ground for the express purpose of making your temporary outside home as comfortable as possible for the day, you sip your brandy milk punch. The creamy concoction soothes your overworked stomach while the brandy gently warms you from the inside out. As soon as that fried chicken works its magic, you'll be fortified for another day of parading.

But now it's summer (or absolutely any season at all), and it's the weekend. You are dressed in your fancy clothes, swaying to the smooth syncopation of a jazz band at brunch.

Your brandy milk punch has the perfect amount of frothy goodness and milky sweetness to complement your eggs Benedict with hollandaise sauce, and life is about as good as it gets. You contemplate ordering a second drink to go along with your Oysters Bienville and your tenderloin slices from the carving station, and you wonder whether a third would be too much to enjoy with your Belgian waffle or bananas foster.

Brandy milk punch completes each of these scenes because not only is it a descendant of one of the oldest cocktails, but also it is arguably one of the most versatile. You need to know about it if you don't already, and even if you are a fan of the Southern version, its origin story is a fascinating one. If you have yet to try brandy milk punch, you're missing out: think of it as a scrumptious, boozy milkshake. And no need to pass on this iconic New Orleans cocktail because you and lactose aren't besties or you're vegan: with a bit of creativity, there is a version for nearly anyone inclined and of legal age. So read on to learn about the history and allure of this fascinating libation that has earned its designation as a classic New Orleans cocktail.

CHAPTER ONE

The Beginnings

ENGLISH MILK PUNCH

> Claret is the liquor for boys; port for men; but he who aspires to be a hero must drink brandy.
>
> —SAMUEL JOHNSON

English milk punch is a clarified beverage that has been around since the seventeenth century. It could be produced in batches and did not require refrigeration, making it a practical choice at a time when drinking spirits was sometimes safer than drinking water. Charles Dickens and Queen Victoria were among the English folks who were crazy about milk punch, but because England was also the place where jellied eels and black pudding were considered tasty treats, that may not be saying much. English, or clarified milk punch, became all the rage in the eighteenth century, was then eclipsed by other alcoholic drinks, and has since experienced a resurgence in the U.S. bar scene. (It is definitely having a moment in New Orleans, where it peacefully coexists alongside its New Orleans–style counterpart.) English milk punch in its most traditional form shares the same ingredients as our beloved brandy milk punch. When making a New Orleans–style brandy milk punch you combine milk with a spirit (often brandy) and sugar or some other sweetener. Sprinkle some grated nutmeg on top, and you're ready to drink up. If you are making the English version, you will have to add citrus to curdle the milk and then strain the mixture before drinking it.

With all the wild variations that mixologists are experimenting with today, English milk punch is more like brandy milk punch's crazy grandpa, but no tale of milk punch would be complete without starting where it all began. And it began across the pond with English milk punch.

Clarified English milk punch (AdobeStock/Brent Hofacker)

BACK TO THE BASICS

People have been consuming alcohol for a very long time—for thousands of years, in fact. Drinking alcohol in ancient times was a way to lower inhibitions and strengthen bonds in society. Not much has changed in almost ten thousand years, at least from this perspective. Once people got a taste for the stuff, they wanted it. Indeed, historians have theorized that we made the transition from hunter-gatherers to farmers not because we wanted food but because we wanted booze. Their evidence includes, among other factors, that food was already plentiful and that the wheat grown by early farmers would have made lousy bread but awesome beer.

We do not know which genius invented alcohol, but we are sure that more than one person made the invention independently. The oldest form of alcohol is credited to China, where residues of a fermented drink of rice, honey, and hawthorn fruit or grapes were found in the archaeological remains of a Neolithic village from 7000 BCE. Wine dates to the Caucasus in 6000 BCE, and the Sumerians get credit for being the first brewmasters in 3000 BCE. In the Americas the Aztecs came up with pulque as early as 1000 BCE; it was made from the fermented sap of agave cactus plants, which is now used to make tequila and mezcal. Clearly, there was a desire for alcohol the world over.

The reasons why people began partaking in alcoholic beverages are as varied as they are fascinating—and are slightly more nuanced than a desire to get sloshed (although this was part of it). Alcohol has many uses. Certainly, there is a medicinal aspect: it has been used as both a stimulant and a sedative. Various types of alcohol were used to cure illnesses or, at the very least, as a vehicle for ingesting less-than-palatable medicines. Before narcotics and chloroform, alcohol was the painkiller of choice. It could take the form of laudanum—an opium and alcohol tincture that was widely used and perfectly legal well into the nineteenth century—or just as a simple swig of whiskey for pain relief in a pinch. Whiskey, in fact, was one of the most popular pain relievers in the United States. Wounded Civil War soldiers were given it for pain management when there were no other drugs available. A 1941

Time Magazine article declared whiskey to be one of the cheapest and best painkillers known to man.

Even during Prohibition, whiskey was prescribed by physicians for a host of ailments and was rubbed on babies' gums to soothe teething discomfort. In a 1920 issue of the *Proceedings of the Royal Society of Medicine,* Dr. Esther Harding sang the praises of alcohol's use for children: "Alcohol is, I suppose, the most valuable sedative and hypnotic drug we possess for infants and young children. Hot toddy as a sleeping draught is good for infants and for the aged." As harmful as this may seem today, it was arguably far more innocuous than the common nineteenth-century practice of giving infants opium tinctures like Mrs. Winslow's Soothing Syrup.

Years past, even if you did not have a toothache or needed a limb chopped off, you might have ingested some form of alcohol for practical purposes. For example, if you were a farmer or had any other kind of physically demanding job in medieval England, chances are you drank beer for breakfast. You didn't do it to get buzzed first thing in the morning but because you needed the calories that beer

Bottle label for Mrs. Winslow's Soothing Syrup, the "mother's friend for children teething" [National Library of Medicine]

provided to perform your duties. You therefore were not drinking a Corona Light with a slice of lime. Instead, you were drinking "small beer," a high-calorie beer with a low alcohol content (typically less than 2.8 percent). There was not enough alcohol in it to get you drunk, but it was a solid choice if you were both thirsty and in need of calories to get through your day—its use was not entirely different from the way people reach for energy drinks today.

Another practical reason to drink alcohol was that it could be a safer option than water. Having access to potable, filtered water was not guaranteed throughout much of human history. There is a bit of myth busting to be done here, however, because historians have refuted the argument that people drank alcohol because it was not safe to drink water. Take early modern England, for example. Most English people then did not avoid drinking water because they feared it was unsafe. Water was cheap and easy to come by, unlike alcohol that either had to be purchased or made/brewed at home. In a time before people knew microorganisms were a thing, there would have been no reason to avoid water so long as it did not smell or taste off. In fact, London invested quite a few pounds in upgrading the city's water duct system during this period. There were regulations about where you were allowed to dump your waste (not in the Thames), even though you could dump it into rivers that emptied into the Thames. Although most people's water was perfectly safe to drink, water sources could sometimes become contaminated or polluted. So, even though it is not necessarily accurate to claim that people thought alcoholic beverages were healthier for them than water, it is true that if the water source was not pure, drinking that water could lead to illness. Plus, alcohol just tasted better.

Of course, not all alcohol was consumed for health reasons or a utilitarian purpose. Social drinking has a long and interesting history, and alcoholic beverages do not get more social than punch. A bowl of punch into which everyone dips a glass (or three) is by its very nature social. Punch, which is produced in batches, is meant to be consumed with others. It is not surprising that punch became a popular drink in eighteenth-century English taverns, pubs, and alehouses. To quote an eighteenth-century ditty, "You may talk of brisk Claret, sing Praises of Sherry, Speak well of old Hock, Mum, Cider and Perry; But you must drink Punch if you mean to be Merry." Punch was clearly epic, but how did it become all the rage in England? Interestingly, this is where the ladies take the stage.

Thomas Rowlandson, *Serving Punch,* c. 1815–20 [Yale Center for British Art, Paul Mellon Collection, B1977.14.319]

LADIES WHO PUNCH

In the preeminent book on all things punch (in case you didn't know there even was such a thing) David Wondrich explains that bartending was women's work: "The mixing of drinks that was done in England in the eighteenth century was not done by men at all. . . . That's not to say that no men ever performed it, but the standard setup was the man as proprietor, host, bouncer, and business manager, while the ones who drew the drinks and served them were female." Thus, women were the ones serving up punch to thirsty patrons.

English milk punch was not just a man's drink—its popularity was certainly helped along by the ladies. During her lifetime, seventeenth-century English playwright and poet Aphra Behn was credited with inventing the beverage, although this is probably not the case. Nevertheless, one of her female characters extols the virtues of punch in *The Widow Ranter:* "Punch! 'Tis my Morning's Draught, my Table-drink, my Treat, my Regalio, my everything." Certainly, both Behn and the Widow Ranter were more than a little fond of their punch.

Women may well have invented the English version of punch or at the very least recorded the recipe for it. One of the earliest surviving milk punch recipes was written by Mary Rockett in 1711. Her recipe called for two gallons of hot milk to be added to a gallon of brandy, five quarts of water, eight lemons, and two pounds of sugar. The mixture should sit for an hour. Because the heat curdled the milk, it could then be strained through cheesecloth, flannel, or whatever was on hand, removing the curds. The result was a clear liquid that required no refrigeration and could last for decades if kept cool. (Bottles of punch were found in Charles Dickens's wine cellar years after his death, and they were reported to be perfectly drinkable.)

English milk punch was not associated with one class of society: women of all stations enjoyed the libation. In fact, Queen Victoria was such a fan that she selected a company, Nathaniel Whisson & Co., to be the official purveyors of milk punch to Her Royal Majesty. She was taking no chances on an inferior punch.

English milk punch made its way across the pond where it was appreciated by women and men alike. Benjamin Franklin, overachiever that he was, came up with his own version, which he included in a letter written to a friend. His recipe packs a wallop, so modern bartenders tone it down. It calls for 6 cups of brandy, eleven lemons, 4 cups of water, 1⅛ cups sugar, one nutmeg, and 3 cups of whole milk (see chapter 5 for the full recipe). Like most English milk punch recipes, this one was neither quick nor easy to prepare. The lemons had to be peeled and steeped in brandy for twenty-four hours. They then had to be juiced, and the milk had to be heated without scorching it and slowly poured over the brandy mixture. After the curds formed, there was a three-step process of letting the mixture sit and then gently stirring it that took an additional two hours. Finally, the punch could be strained (twice). Benjamin Franklin was by all accounts a busy man, but he liked his punch enough to record and share this time-consuming recipe.

It requires patience to make an English milk punch. As the world industrialized, this drink fell out of favor, and easier-to-make libations became popular for several reasons. Techniques for aging and distilling liquors improved, so alcohol needed less fiddling with to improve its taste. It was no longer necessary to use the milk curds to soften the harsh flavors of early modern liquors when the taste of the liquors themselves had become more palatable by the nineteenth century. Individually prepared cocktails eventually supplanted communal bowls of punch, except for the occasional party or holiday gathering.

LET'S BE CLEAR: CLARIFIED PUNCH IS STILL A THING

Although English milk punch might have gone out of fashion in the nineteenth century, it still lives on. It has, in fact, enjoyed a recent resurgence in places like New York City. In the early twenty-first century, bartenders started rediscovering and tinkering with this historic cocktail. Rather than making bowls of the stuff, some are condensing the punch into single-glass drinks, while others are sticking with the traditional batch method. Some mixologists are experimenting like mad scientists, making cutting-edge recipes. (We've seen everything from tom yum soup to Fruity Pebble milk included.) These out-of-the-box thinkers are creating clarified milk punches whose descriptions range from the wacky to the sublime. Taking a centuries-old cocktail recipe, and revamping it with modern ingredient combinations, yields a fascinating drink.

Often, people making modern English milk punches no longer use warm milk and instead substitute cooking acids for the lemons. The process is still time consuming, however. In fact, it takes even longer—about three days—using the cold milk method. Yet there is something magical about straining the gelatinous, clumpy milk curdles and being left with a creamy but clear liquid. And the magic continues when you sip a liquid that looks like water but is full of vibrant, sometimes exotic, flavor.

Although the process takes longer with cold milk, it results in a more consistent drink. Using cooking acids rather than citrus to curdle the milk means that flavor possibilities are limitless for modern-day clarified milk punches. Because the process of straining the curds softens the flavors, mixologists can really get imaginative with their ingredient combinations. One of the appeals of clarified milk punch today is its versatility. You can use any kind of milk, from half and half, to cream, to soy or almond, or coconut milk. You can also use any spirit, juice, or tea. (See chapter 5 for recipe ideas.) The sky's the limit: the only boundaries are your creativity.

Of course, New York is not the only place rediscovering and reinventing English milk punch. New Orleans loves a cocktail, and there are always adventurous mixologists pushing the envelope and making the old new again. The rest of this book is about New Orleans–style brandy milk punch, but if you want to try an English (or clarified) milk punch in New Orleans, you have many options. Try the Empire Bar at Broussard's for a traditional English milk punch. Or try Saffron Nola. Order the "Easy Money" cocktail and you will get a clarified cocktail made with yogurt and tequila.

Milk punch is a classic cocktail with a long history and a promising future, and because there is nothing that New Orleans mixologists like more than giving a classic cocktail a new twist, it will probably remain a popular choice for years to come. But New Orleans–style milk punch is the true classic here. It has become the unofficial brunch (throughout the year) and seasonal drink of the city. It too has a fascinating story that is as captivating as the city that serves it—one that should not have made it out of infancy but went on to thrive, despite natural disasters, war, and epidemics, to be a hub for entertainment and revelry (and of course, for the most excellent milk punch).

CHAPTER TWO

New Orleans Cocktail History

An American monkey, after getting drunk on brandy, would never touch it again, and thus is much wiser than most men.

—CHARLES DARWIN

Understanding the drinking culture in New Orleans begins with understanding the city's attitude toward alcohol in general. Alcoholic beverages are consumed regularly, and what is consumed depends more on traditions than on trends. New Orleans has always marched to its own beat and has never been concerned much with following what other cities are doing. Traditional cocktails like the Vieux Carré and Ramos Gin Fizz will always be served, but new cocktails are constantly being created whether they are trendy or not. In New Orleans alcohol is served 24/7: there is no last call. Day drinking and getting a go-cup from a bar (as long as you are only walking) are not frowned on, especially during Carnival season. There's no judgment here. That's because drinking is accepted as part of the celebration of life, not a way to get away from it. Cocktails are imbibed to share good times with friends and family, not to forget the bad times. And the purpose of drinking is not to get drunk. Perhaps the French heritage helps explain the attitude in New Orleans toward drinking alcohol. The French savor their wine, drinking it slowly. Pacing is important. After all, what's the point of having a good time if you cannot remember it the next day?

The lack of concern for trends holds true in many aspects of life here, not just cocktails. It is a big part of what makes this city unique. We do not have to work to stay weird—it happens naturally. New Orleans buries her dead with music and dancing. Most people here do not make

New Year's resolutions about losing weight or exercising. Just the opposite happens. Every year from the start of Carnival season on January 6 (Twelfth Night) through the day before Ash Wednesday (Shrove Tuesday or Mardi Gras Day), the whole city celebrates. The partying intensifies in the two weeks leading up to Mardi Gras Day. Then everything ends exactly at midnight, making way for repentance and fasting during the forty days of Lent. The four seasons here are not winter, spring, summer, and fall: they are Carnival, festival, hurricane, and football. New Orleans is under no threat of losing its weirdness ever. Let's all drink to that!

A DUBIOUS LOCATION

To understand New Orleans cocktail history, you must know a little bit about the history of this 300+-year-old city. The area that is now New Orleans was originally inhabited by Native Americans as early as 1000 BCE. In the 1690s fur trappers and traders reached the area. Later, the

French founded a city here. Considering the initial placement of the French colony of Nouvelle Orléans—on a foreign continent, barely above (and in many places below) sea level in an area surrounded by marshes and pestered by mosquitos, alligators, and poisonous snakes—it is somewhat of a miracle that the colony survived at all. But survive it did. That colony, once a small outpost on the banks of the Mississippi River (then known as the St. Louis River), thrived and is now New Orleans, Louisiana, the most unique and European of all American cities.

THE FIRST MARDI GRAS

In 1682, during the French colonial period in the New World, Robert Cavelier de LaSalle claimed for France all the land drained by the great river on which he traveled south from Canada to the Gulf of Mexico. LaSalle named the river the St. Louis River and christened the land "Louisiana" in honor of the French king Louis XIV. Of course, claiming land is different from owning it, and the king of

France realized that if the French did not occupy the area, he would lose it—along with his dream of an empire in the New World. Enter the brothers Pierre LeMoyne, Sieur d' Iberville and Jean Baptiste LeMoyne, Sieur de Bienville. They were sent to establish a colony in Louisiana along the St. Louis (Mississippi) River. After surviving a night of heavy storms, the expedition landed at the mouth of the river on March 2, 1699. That date happened to be Shrove Tuesday (Mardi Gras), the day before Ash Wednesday. A rest from the treacherous journey was in order: Shrove Tuesday was a reason to celebrate.

TRICKSTERS

Bienville understood the need to colonize the territory and create outposts to maintain French control of the land. He was exploring the lower Mississippi valley when on September 15, 1699, he encountered a shipload of British colonizers in the river looking to establish a settlement. The British captain asked for directions. Bienville told him he was in the wrong waterway and that the river was much farther to the west. The British captain fell for the bluff, turned around, and headed back out into the Gulf of Mexico. (Could this have been the beginning of the reluctance of men to ask for directions?) Another cause for celebration and a cocktail! That point in the Mississippi River is still known as English Turn.

THE BIRTH OF A LEGENDARY CITY

In 1718, Bienville settled on a spot in the crescent of the river to build his city. This spot was chosen partly because it was near a Native American portage that made it easier to get into the Gulf of Mexico by way of backwaters, including Bayou St. John and what is now Lake Pontchartrain, Lake Maurepas, and Lake Borne. This route eliminated the need to navigate the mouth of the river, a very dangerous and often catastrophic sailing adventure. It was also the place where the river is closest to the lake. Bienville was assured that, by situating the city in the crescent

Exterior of Pat O'Brien's Courtyard Restaurant and Bar in the Vieux Carré

of the river, hurricanes and tidal waves could be avoided. A more inaccurate weather prediction cannot be imagined, considering that modern-day New Orleanians stock up on necessary supplies, including fine spirits, every year in early June in preparation for hurricane season, which runs until November 30. "Hurricane" is not only a season here, but it is also a popular alcoholic beverage. The Hurricane cocktail, a rum-based drink served in a glass shaped like a hurricane lamp, was invented by Pat O'Brien's bar. In the 1940s rum was easier to get than whiskey or scotch, so the bartenders at Pat O's came up with the Hurricane. Any bartender in town will mix up a Hurricane for you: it is one of the classic New Orleans cocktails. But the best place to drink one is in the courtyard of Pat O's. While you are there, you may stick with the weather theme because they also make a Cyclone and a Rainstorm cocktail.

In 1721, the original city streets of New Orleans were laid on a grid in what now makes up the Vieux Carré or French Quarter. Many of the streets were named for Catholic saints and royal houses of France. One of those royal houses was the House of Bourbon. It is not surprising that almost all visitors mistakenly think Bourbon Street was named after an alcoholic spirit, given the number of bars on it.

A CONFEDERACY OF CHARACTERS

Convincing people to settle in Nouvelle Orléans was no easy task for Bienville. John Law, who had control of the settlement, marketed it to French citizens as the Paris of the New World where they could easily collect gold and pearls. He promised a moderate climate and fertile soil for farming. Even with this utopian description, Law found it difficult to convince Frenchmen to settle in Louisiana. He therefore began importing prisoners, prostitutes, and paupers by nefarious means to increase the population. This gave New Orleans the unfortunate reputation of a city with loose morals. That would in part be corrected by the Ursuline nuns who came over in 1727 to bring religion and some degree of decorum to the city. Yet, as the city grew and developed a more acceptable culture, it retained some of its scruffiness and individuality. Those elements are still part of the culture.

The Spanish ruled New Orleans from 1763 to just before the Louisiana Purchase in 1803. Because of the destructive fires during the French colonial period, much of the architecture of the French Quarter is Spanish. Adding to the mix of cultures were African, Caribbean, and Latin American influences. This diversity created unique traditions and celebrations, resulting in a joyful way of living or, as the French call it, *joie de vivre*. The *joie de vivre* that exists in New Orleans today is also a result of Pierre Cavag-

King and queen of a Mardi Gras ball (Okeanos, 2022)

nal de Rigaud, Marquis de Vaudreuil, who in 1743 replaced Bienville as governor of Louisiana. The marquis brought an extravagant and unprecedented frivolity to the city. He and his wife lavishly entertained, giving state dinner feasts served on plates of solid gold. It was during this time that the city of New Orleans began to celebrate Mardi Gras with the French tradition of masked balls and revelry that preceded the forty days of fasting during Lent. The traditions of constant celebrations and festivals we have today in New Orleans no doubt grew from seeds sown during the administration of the marquis.

NEW ORLEANS COCKTAIL CULTURE

One of the main reasons why New Orleans has a strong cocktail culture today is that it has always been here and never went away. New Orleans's history includes Storyville, a legal red-light district and the home of many brothels and bars. The city was also once a center for the operations of pirates and privateers. Neither the "Noble Experiment" of Prohibition nor the banning of absinthe altered New Orleanians' attitudes toward imbibing in spirits.

By the time the Americans arrived in 1803, New Orleanians were just too entrenched in their own culture to adapt to the stricter rules of behavior and attitude toward partying and drinking adhered to by the American/English population. What the Americans may have considered debauchery and overindulgence, New Orleanians considered acceptable, even desirable, behavior, reasoning that we are only here for a short time and there is a lot to celebrate in life. The commonly heard phrase, "Everywhere they eat to live, in New Orleans we live to eat," exemplifies this attitude toward indulgence.

The dichotomy of New Orleanians' attitude toward overindulgence and traditional reverence is most evident in the difference between Mardi Gras and Ash Wednesday. Contrast the unbridled raucous celebration of Mardi Gras with the somber observance of Ash Wednesday, and you see the two faces of New Orleans culture. Even today, the police clear the streets of the French Quarter on Mardi Gras night at exactly midnight. The time for enjoying life is over, and it is now time to repent. Yesterday's partygoers enter St. Louis Cathedral on Ash Wednesday morning to be reminded that we will all return to ashes someday: it is time for forty days of Lent.

Interior of St. Louis Cathedral in New Orleans

PIRATES IN A PORT CITY

Since its inception, New Orleans has been a major port city because of its placement on the Mississippi River, the main highway from north to south in the New World. The amount of traffic passing through the port lured pirates and privateers, most notably Jean Lafitte and his brother Pierre, who operated a robust smuggling trade in the French Quarter. A humble blacksmith shop located on the corner of Bourbon and St. Philip Streets was believed to be the center of their operations in the early nineteenth century. Lafitte's Blacksmith Shop is also one of the oldest structures (if not the oldest) still used as a bar in the United States.

Apparently, Jean Lafitte approves of this continued use because it is reported that his ghost still frequents the place. When you drop in for a voodoo daiquiri, just ask long-time bartender Jason Robards what he has seen. The building has been home to rum drinking since the eighteenth century and does not seem to be slowing down any time soon.

In the more recent past, New Orleans's position as a major port bringing in sailors from all over the world seeking the pleasure of a woman's company led to the establishment of Storyville, a legal red-light district on January 1, 1898. Alcoholic beverages flowed freely in that neighborhood. Tom Anderson, the unofficial mayor of Storyville,

Lafitte's Blacksmith Shop on Bourbon Street in the French Quarter

owned and operated a saloon/brothel that was also used as a tourist information center and an unofficial courthouse on Basin Street. A must-see for any visitor to Storyville was the magnificent cherrywood bar that stretched for a half-block and boasted five huge arched mirrors, which was the centerpiece of Anderson's Annex Cafe and Chop House. The U.S. Navy shut down Storyville in 1917, but the legacy of jazz music that began and thrived there lives on in the culture and rhythm of New Orleans.

PHARMACISTS AND APOTHECARIES

As mentioned, the use of alcohol for medicinal purposes was a common practice in the eighteenth and nineteenth centuries. It was often used as a general anesthetic, but it also served curative and preventive purposes. Brandy and whiskey were used the most, and physicians and pharmacists prescribed them often for children, as well as adults. In 1816 Louis J. Dufilho Jr., a resident of New Orleans, became the first licensed pharmacist in the country. He set up his apothecary in the French Quarter. The Pharmacy Museum at 514 Chartres Street is a tribute to his legacy and provides a stunning—and sometimes terrifying—glimpse into the methods used by pharmacists in the nineteenth century.

Over the last two hundred years pharmacists have also made significant contributions to New Orleans cocktail history. The pharmacist and apothecary proprietor who is most famous in the history of New Orleans cocktails, Antoine Amédée Peychaud, created Peychaud's Bitters in the 1800s. These bitters had a strong anise flavor and a hint of mint and are the essential ingredient in the official New Orleans cocktail, the Sazerac. Peychaud mixed his bitters with Sazerac-de-Forge et fils, a French brandy, in the first Sazerac recipe. Rye whiskey later replaced brandy, and a few dashes of absinthe (or an absinthe rinse of the glass) were added to produce the contemporary recipe.

Absinthe has always been culturally associated with New Orleans. The city introduced absinthe to the country and was the most popular place in America to drink it until it was banned in the United States in 1912 because it was believed to be hallucinogenic. Even after the Twenty-First Amendment was passed, ending Prohibition, the ban on absinthe continued for almost a century. Of course, this ban necessitated development of a substitute. That came in the form of Herbsaint, an anise-flavored liqueur created by J. Marion Legendre in 1934. Legendre was a New Orleans apothecary proprietor and entrepreneur who learned about absinthe and pastis, a French anise-flavored liqueur, while serving in France during World War I. After Prohibition ended, Legendre made and sold his liqueur under the name "Legendre Absinthe." Soon, the Federal Alcohol Control Administration forced him to remove absinthe from the product. He changed the name to Herbsaint, the French term for "sacred herb." In 1949 he sold his company to Sazerac, which still produces the product.

Considering that several classic cocktails like the Sazarac, the Ramos Gin Fizz, the Absinthe Frappé, the Roffignac, the Cocktail à la Louisiane, the Vieux Carré, the Café Brûlot, and the Hurricane were all created here, this city is a required visit for any cocktail enthusiast. And yet the brandy milk punch probably does not top the list of "must-tries" when tourists visit the city. After all, it's no Hurricane, and most people would probably opt for a Bloody Mary when looking for a quintessential day drink in New Orleans. Yet, even though a Bloody Mary here is sublime, there is a case to be made for branching out and trying a brandy milk punch if you are not already a connoisseur. You may just find yourself won over by its charms.

CHAPTER THREE

Punch-Drunk in NOLA

NEW ORLEANS BRANDY MILK PUNCH

Alcoholic drinks, rightly used, are good for body and soul alike, but as a restorative of both there is nothing like brandy.

—GEORGE SAINTSBURY

The New Orleans version of milk punch is an innocuous, wholesome-looking drink that starts out delicate and frothy but then packs a punch (pardon the pun). Traditional brandy milk punch has only a few key ingredients: brandy, sugar (usually powdered), nutmeg, milk, and ice.

It is certainly an example of the sum being greater than its parts, but the stories behind the parts are undoubtedly interesting.

New Orleans–style brandy milk punch is a cocktail that is most often enjoyed during the daylight hours. It is typically a breakfast/lunch/brunch libation. If you have not had the pleasure of tasting one, it may seem odd to drink brandy first thing in the morning, because brandy is often considered a digestif. However, taking a nip of brandy in the morning is a time-honored tradition for ensuring good health. Brandy milk punch is a hair-of-the-dog, defogging-the-brain, get-going-after-a-night-out sort of cocktail. Could there be some medicinal truth behind these claims? Interestingly, every single one of the ingredients in a New Orleans-style brandy milk punch has some medicinal value associated with it. Together they make a festive, fun cocktail that might just cure whatever ails you—or, if not, might make you forget you were feeling bad in the first place.

Brandy was first distilled in medieval France for medicinal purposes. It was dubbed (some say by physicians, others by monks) *eau-de-vie* (the water of life) because of its healing powers. Physicians were still prescribing brandy in the twentieth century for use as a stimulant (particularly to revive people from fainting spells), a sedative (as a sleep aid to calm anxiety and to soothe colicky infants), and a fever reducer. Depending on the distillation method, brandy may share some of the same health benefits of red wine. People have lauded brandy for its ability to do everything from boost the immune system to prevent cancer and soothe a sore throat. It also contains high levels of vitamin C. And brandy was touted in the medical journal *The Lancet* as "universally regarded as superior to all other spirits from a medicinal point of view."

Brandy proved especially helpful for people on the go. The word *brandy* is a shortened form of *brandywine,* from the Dutch word meaning "burnt wine." This is a reference to sixteenth-century Dutch sailors who boiled barrels of French wine to reduce its weight, thereby lightening the ship's load. Brandy became a necessity not just for sailors but also for explorers. For instance, "medicinal" brandy was a must on packing lists during the heroic age of Antarctic exploration, 1897–1922. One such explorer complained in a diary entry that the expedition leader had consumed all the brandy: "Unless the doctor has a bottle or so, we have not a drop of brandy at Cape Adair for medicinal purposes. On this occasion we were obliged to use whiskey. It is really scandalous." A physician on another expedition lamented, "For the second year there were only very few bottles left, which were reserved for festive occasions or for medical use." Brandy was a coveted commodity on these journeys.

Even when weight and space were not issues, the demand for brandy skyrocketed: it became the spirit of choice across Europe for hundreds of years. Brandy's popularity spread to the American colonies, where it was made not just from grapes but also from whatever fruit was handy, such as apples, pears, or peaches. Brandy became so popular, in fact, that it is credited with transforming spirits from predominantly medicinal products into the main ingredients of the cocktails we now enjoy. Whisky, gin, and rum have the brandy trade to thank for their popularity.

Cocktails themselves started out as medicinal. In the nineteenth century—and indeed, well before then—you popped over to your local apothecary (or pharmacy) to get your medicine. There was a good chance you would be given brandy and bitters, depending on your ailment. If this sounds an awful lot like a cocktail, that's because it is. At its core, a cocktail is a mixture of spirits, sugar, bitters, and water. There are many tall tales about the origin of the term "cocktail." One is that it originated in New Orleans with Antoine Amedée Peychaud, owner of an apothecary shop and creator of Peychaud's Bitters, as described in chapter 2. The story goes that in 1838 he made brandy drinks for his friends. To incorporate his bitters into the drink, he used a double-ended egg cup, known as a "coquetier" in place of a jigger. The word was Americanized, and eventually the concoction was called a cocktail. Although the word "cocktail" did not actually originate this way, the Sazerac cocktail—consisting of Sazerac brandy and Peychaud's Bitters—did become the first branded cocktail in 1853.

Although Sazeracs are now typically made with rye whiskey in place of brandy, you can still enjoy Sazerac de Forge & Fils Cognac. A quick note on brandy: every Cognac is a brandy, but not all brandy is a Cognac. Cognac is a type of brandy from the Cognac region of southwestern France. It is made with a very specific type of grapes and undergoes two rounds of distillation in a strict process. Sazerac describes the tasting notes of its Cognac as rich and floral, distinctly creamy in texture, showing hints of exotic spice on the palate, and having a long, soft finish and a hint of natural sweetness. It is a delicious choice for a brandy milk punch. Of course, brandy is the star of this cocktail, but the other ingredients have interesting tales to tell as well. You cannot have a proper milk punch without a sweetener, and Louisiana sugar is the perfect complement to a New Orleans–style brandy milk punch.

LOUISIANA SUGAR

Sugarcane as a crop in New Orleans dates to 1751 when Jesuit priests planted it at the site of the present-day Immaculate Conception Church in the central business district. Before it became a main cash crop in New Orleans, indigo and tobacco were the crops of choice. This began to change in the late eighteenth century when Étienne de Boré converted his plantation crop from indigo to sugar. His plantation, which sits on the current location of Audubon Park, was experiencing financial difficulties, so he took a chance on growing sugar instead. And it was definitely a gamble. Louisiana is the northernmost latitude where sugar is grown. As hot as summer can get here, it is not a tropical environment (it's subtropical); the growing season is therefore shorter, and frosts can potentially ruin crops during the harvest season, which runs from October through December.

The gamble paid off because Antoine Morin, a chemist and a free man of color originally from Saint-Domingue, developed a process to granulate sugar on Boré's plantation. This innovation jump-started the sugar industry in Louisiana. Within ten years of the granulation breakthrough, more than seventy sugar plantations lined the banks of the Mississippi River. The sugar industry became so successful that it hastened Louisiana's admittance to the United States.

While sugar cultivation proved an economic boom for plantation owners, it had a decidedly negative effect on enslaved people. Harvesting and processing sugar are very labor-intensive processes, made even more so in Louisiana because of the shortened growing season. To ensure that the sugarcane was harvested before the first frost, slaves were forced to work tirelessly on sugar plantations. Sugarcane production created a need for large numbers of enslaved people, which contributed to New Orleans becoming a hub for domestic slave trading in the nineteenth century. Close to one million slaves would be transferred to the lower South, often through the New Orleans slave market, to work Louisiana's sugarcane and cotton fields.

By the mid-nineteenth century the area known as the "sugar bowl" (from the lower Mississippi River to Natchitoches and west to Opelousas) was producing 105,000 tons of sugarcane; by 1861 this output more than doubled to 230,000 tons. Production plummeted dramatically during the Civil War and slowly built up again after emancipation, when new labor sources were found. Sugarcane remains to this day an important part of the state's economy. The American Sugar Cane League estimates the overall economic impact at $3 billion per year. Louisiana sugar growers harvest fifteen million tons of sugarcane and produce 1.6 million tons of raw sugar annually, and more than 17,000 people work in sugarcane processing and production in the state. One iconic local sugar company, the Domino Sugar Refinery in Chalmette, Louisiana—a few miles downriver from New Orleans—has been in operation since 1909 and refines seven million pounds of sugar each day. It is the largest cane sugar refinery in the Western Hemisphere. It closes one day a year—Mardi Gras Day—so its four hundred employees can enjoy copious amounts of the sugary goodness central to the holiday, king cake.

A king cake is a traditional Carnival treat baked from January 6 (Twelfth Night or King's Day) through Mardi Gras Day. It can be a simple brioche, a cinnamon roll, or a filled coffee cake. What's important is that it is decorated with purple, yellow, and green sugar and contains a plastic baby. Whoever gets the slice with the baby has to buy the next king cake, give a party, or both.

A word about powdered sugar (or confectioners' sugar or icing sugar), which many brandy milk punch recipes specify. The process of developing powdered sugar dates to at least the seventeenth century (and some argue even earlier), when refined sugar was sifted to separate large crystals from finer ones. By the nineteenth century, sugar was grinded and sifted into a fine powder—what we would consider today to be powdered sugar. Powdered sugar is not technically the same as confectioners' sugar, although the names are often used interchangeably. Confectioners' sugar has an added ingredient, cornstarch, used to prevent the sugar from clumping. All confectioners' sugar contains cornstarch, so if you do not want this ingredient in your drink, opt for powdered sugar. And just to confuse the matter a bit more, Canadians and Brits use the term "icing sugar" because powdered sugar is used to make icing.

We would be remiss if we discussed powdered sugar and neglected to mention what might arguably be its most iconic use—heaped on top of beignets, sometimes referred to as powdered sugar pillows. The ancestor of the beignet dates to the ancient Romans, who first fried up dough and

Beignets topped with powdered sugar [AdobeStock/Adam Lorber]

found it delectable. Much later, the French perfected the technique of frying dough, and these little goodies made their way to New Orleans in the seventeenth century. Some say they migrated with French Canadian settlers who came to Louisiana, and others credit the Ursuline nuns. Regardless of how they found their way to NOLA, they are entrenched here now (thank goodness).

While sugar-coated beignets are not considered to be good for you (although you could argue they are good for the soul), sugar was prized for its medicinal use in ancient Greece and Rome. By the mid-twelfth century, Europeans used sugar to treat everything from a cough to a stomach-ache. Regardless of its medical efficacy, ingesting sugar made people feel better because they enjoyed eating it. So even after sugar was no longer considered in and of itself a cure for ailments, its use in medicine continued because it had a practical application: it was a vehicle to make the bitter-tasting medicines of the day more palatable. As Mary Poppins sings, a spoonful of the stuff will help the medicine go down. And before the twentieth century medicine was not palatable on its own. Before the mass production of easy-to-swallow pills, pill making was time consuming and expensive. Therefore, medicine was usually administered in liquid or powdered form. If you have ever tried to get your kid to drink medicine, you know what a struggle it can be (thank goodness for bubble-gum–flavored amoxicillin). Bitter medicine was mixed with pure sugar and eventually with sweet syrups (this is where Hershey's syrup got its start) and carbonated drinks like Coca Cola, which originally contained cocaine and was considered to be a healthy stimulant. Sugar, due in part to its myriad uses in food, drinks, and medicines, became a prized commodity. But there is another ingredient in brandy milk punch that was prized equally, if not more.

NUTMEG

Nutmeg is not a nut: it is a seed, and it has a wild tale to tell. Although the full story is beyond the scope of this book, the short version is that people fought wars over this precious seed. They thought it could cure everything from plague to hemorrhoids to memory loss. At one time nutmeg was literally worth more than its weight in gold. It is also not hyperbole to suggest that some went nuts for nutmeg, especially because it is also considered a hallucinogenic.

Nutmeg is the seed kernel inside the fruit of the nutmeg tree. It is native to the Maluku Islands of Indonesia (formerly the Spice Islands). The ancient Egyptians used nutmeg seed oil for embalming and as incense. Arab merchants brought nutmeg to Constantinople as early as the sixth century. Nutmeg reached the apex of its popularity in the sixteenth century after the Portuguese discovered it, and Western Europeans got on the nutmeg bandwagon. It became a coveted and expensive spice and was considered one of the most prized luxury items of the century, in large part because of its perceived medicinal properties. Westerners used nutmeg both as preventive medicine and as a cure for a wide variety of ailments.

The demand for this rare spice led to several wars during the sixteenth century, with Venice, Genoa, the Netherlands, Portugal, and England all fighting over it. Arguably the Dutch were the craziest for nutmeg. In their yearning to control nutmeg production, they killed and enslaved the inhabitants of the nutmeg-producing island of Banda, and in 1667 they traded the island of Manhattan to the British in return for the nutmeg-growing Indonesian island of Run.

There was also a fair bit of superstition and folklore surrounding nutmeg. Nutmeg was believed to protect against evil in general and, in some cases, specific unfortunate outcomes. For instance, if you received a nutmeg at the new year and kept it in your pocket, you were protected from breaking a bone. If you placed your trusty nutmeg under your armpit (the left one), you could attract people to you, possibly even a mate. These mystical qualities surrounding nutmeg persisted in some places well into the nineteenth century. The spice was still so prized at that time that Charles Dickens was known to carry his personalized nutmeg grater in his waistcoat.

Grating nutmeg has become the most common way to enjoy the spice, whether in a baked fall treat or sprinkled atop an adult beverage. Either way, the warm, earthy flavor with that touch of sweetness perfectly complements milky beverages like brandy milk punch. Just do not ingest nutmeg in large quantities: it contains myristicin, a hallucinogen that can produce mind-altering effects, not dissimilar to LSD. Who knew that cozy little nutmeg that gives you those Christmastime feels has a darker side?

MILK

Although milk may not have a flashy backstory like nutmeg, it is an essential component of our cocktail. You simply cannot have a brandy milk punch without the milk, and unlike the English version, we like to keep our milk front and center in our punch, in all its uncurdled glory. One interesting local connection is that Louis Armstrong worked in the New Orleans milk industry in his youth. When he was fourteen years old, he began full-time employment as a delivery boy on a horse-drawn milk wagon for the Cloverland Dairy in New Orleans. In his autobiography, Armstrong recalls that on payday he and the other delivery boys would go around the corner from the dairy and start a big craps game with their newly earned funds.

Milkman with mule-drawn wagon [The Charles L. Franck Studio Collection at The Historic New Orleans Collection, Acc. No. 1979.325.4062]

Like all our ingredients, milk was believed to have medicinal qualities throughout history. The very earliest physicians, such as Hippocrates, Galen, and Pliny, used raw milk to cure everything from tuberculosis to constipation. In the nineteenth century raw milk was still being consistently used by physicians to treat an array of disorders; it was thought of as particularly effective for ulcers and other gastric complaints. In the early twentieth century Dr. J. R. Crewe, founder of the Mayo Foundation, created the Milk Cure, which dictated that patients drink copious amounts of raw milk for a prescribed number of weeks. The Milk Cure was reported to alleviate, if not cure, illnesses ranging from cancer to nerve and brain disorders. Doctors believed that raw milk improved the quality of their patients' blood.

Medicinal attributes aside, the drinking of cow's milk was entrenched in American society. The demand to produce milk therefore led to a booming dairy industry. New Orleans, like most major cities, had a dairy belt, a rural area where land was cheap and plentiful for cows to graze but near enough to transport fresh milk to the city. In the 1700s and early 1800s, New Orleans's dairy products came from

Cloverland Dairy railroad car (The Charles L. Franck Studio Collection at The Historic New Orleans Collection, Acc. No. 1979.325.2855)

farms along Bayou Road and Metairie and Gentilly Ridges, and sometimes from plantations close to the city. In the mid-nineteenth century, railroads enabled dairy farmers to send their wares far more rapidly than by wagon or by water: milk could travel quickly in refrigerated railroad cars and arrive in the city from outlying areas in only a few hours. By the twentieth century, railroads had shifted New Orleans's main dairy belt all the way across Lake Pontchartrain to the parishes (counties) of Washington, St. Helena, and Tangipahoa. Tangipahoa Parish was shipping two thousand gallons of milk per day to New Orleans by 1910. This dairy belt boom was also made possible by ice. Ice-cooled refrigerated rail cars made transporting milk sixty miles away from the city possible. Trains could travel through hot, steamy swamps to deliver fresh milk daily to the city of New Orleans. Ice also made the cocktail what it is today.

ICE

Where would the cocktail world be without ice? It is hard to imagine a recipe that does not call for ice in some form. Whether it's ice balls (you can freeze them with your initials for your own personalized cubes), Collins Spears, crushed ice, or standard cubes, ice makes the drink. Exacting mixologists are quite particular about what kind and quantity of ice should be used in making and serving their cocktails.

And of course, there is a medicinal aspect to ice. The Egyptians were using cold to soothe injuries and decrease inflammation as early as 2500 BCE. A millennium later we have evidence, written on papyrus, that Egyptians were engaging in cryotherapy, the use of cold temperatures to treat disease. Hippocrates prescribed the use of cold treatment to alleviate swelling and pain in 400 BCE. Napoleon's surgeon used it to facilitate amputations. In the mid-nineteenth century physicians in England were touting the benefits of cold application to treat migraines. Eventually cryosurgery would be developed to treat various skin cancers and skin disorders.

While ice has been helping people the world over for millennia, it has enabled New Orleanians to stay cool with a cocktail since at least the early 1800s. Nineteenth-century folks had one man to thank above all others for bringing ice to the sweltering South: Frederic Tudor, the

"Ice King" (1783–1864). Tudor started a business harvesting ice from frozen ponds in New England and developed a way to ship it southward. By the 1830s he was packing large quantities of Massachusetts ice in sawdust, loading it aboard ships, and sending it down South and eventually to far-away places like Europe, the Caribbean, and even British India. Henry David Thoreau, after observing Tudor's workers chipping away at Walden Pond, penned the line, "The pure Walden water is mingled with the sacred water of the Ganges." By the 1850s, Frederic Tudor was shipping fifty thousand tons of ice all over the world, including to New Orleans, where Tudor owned one of the many ice houses that dotted the city. These warehouses stored ice until it could be shipped throughout New Orleans, making ice more readily obtainable and increasing its popularity.

The demand for ice in New Orleans (and the rest of the country) grew throughout the nineteenth century. People wanted to keep their food and medicines chilled, as well as their cocktails. In 1862 Jerry Thomas published *The Bartenders Guide,* the first serious book on cocktails and punches. Most of the recipes called for ice, which in-

Horse-drawn ice wagon on Royal Street in the French Quarter (The Historic New Orleans Collection, Acc. No. 2001.56.72)

dicates that Americans were accustomed to having their drinks served chilled by then. Artificial refrigeration would eventually negate the need for transporting natural ice. (The first commercial ice maker was invented in 1854.) Ice became big business in New Orleans, not only because it can be hot as the hinges on the gates of Hades but also because New Orleanians like a cold cocktail. Since necessity is the mother of invention, it is not surprising that the world's first documented commercial ice production facility was in New Orleans, on Tchoupitoulas Street. Louisiana Ice Works opened for large-scale commercial business in 1868, although it had been producing ice at least since 1865, ensuring that even on a sweltering August afternoon in the Crescent City, you could get your brandy milk punch chilled and poured over ice. Now that is better living through science!

Brandy, sugar, nutmeg, milk, ice: each ingredient in a brandy milk punch has a history, and each has a tradition of being used for medicinal purposes, much like the origins of the cocktail in general. So, the next time you find yourself at brunch enjoying that classic New Orleans–style brandy milk punch, take a minute to recall the backstories of its ingredients. Then enjoy the perfect symphony of flavor notes of these combined ingredients and make a toast to everyone's health!

CHAPTER FOUR

Brunch Punch

NEW ORLEANS BRUNCH CULTURE

If brandy was made out of sparrows, there would soon be no sparrows.

—GEORGE LICHTENBERG

Which is better, breakfast food or lunch food? The debate has raged almost as long as humans settled on three meals per day. The answer is both. Why choose? Brunch culture has exploded in recent years in cities across the country, and New Orleans is at its epicenter. Pairing the perfect libation with seemingly never-ending food choices is practically an art form, but there are a few mainstays. The Sazerac is widely accepted as the official drink of New Orleans, but at least for part of the year, and at certain times of the day, it has a rival. The brandy milk punch cocktail makes its presence known around Christmas and New Year's Eve celebrations and all year round at brunch. The creamy, frothy, fragrant booziness of the drink makes an excellent accompaniment to the vast array of brunch food choices. This chapter explores the cocktail's well-earned place in New Orleans brunch culture.

BREAKFAST, LUNCH, BRUNCH, AND BLUNCH: WHERE DID IT ALL BEGIN?

In simplest terms, brunch is a six-letter word that combines two meals: breakfast and lunch. But in real life brunch opens a world of delectable possibilities. It is not exactly clear when or where brunch originated or how it spread. Many believe its origins were in nineteenth-century England with the tradition of the hunting feast. At that time, hunting was a favorite pastime of the upper classes. It continues in modern times with modifications and with some exceptions to the ban on hunting imposed by Parliament's Hunting Act of 2004. The British make a clear distinction between hunting and shooting. Hunting is the pursuit of animals with hounds, most commonly fox hunting, whereas shooting involves game birds, usually pheasants, on a large estate. Clearly, both activities call for some significant sustenance afterward.

Historically, the morning hunt would start with a slice of fruitcake or some eggs and fruit set out on a table on the lawn. At some point, that tradition gave way to an after-the-hunt feast. Dining room tables were set with fine linens, bone china, and crystal stemware. Bowls of fresh flowers added color and fragrance to the room. Sideboards held large silver chafing dishes filled with breakfast and lunch fare, including eggs, sausages, ham, fruits, sweets, and breads, and, of course, libations. By the 1890s the dishes also included various game birds. This hearty fare was just what was needed to replenish the body after a long ride atop a horse. The hunt and the ensuing feasts were festive, elegant, and opulent. It is no wonder that these events are so often depicted in paintings of the period.

The hunting and the after-the-hunt feast traditions found their way to North America, although they fell somewhat out of favor after the Revolutionary War. Nevertheless, fox hunting and the hunt breakfast are still part of life on both sides of the pond. With dishes like catfish stew, alligator stew, and country captain chicken set out on the table, we can safely say the menu is a bit different on the American side of the pond.

The hunting feast could easily have been the beginning of brunch, but there are other theories about its origins. Some say brunch stems from the Catholic tradition of fasting before Sunday mass and the need for a substantial meal afterward. Fasting began on midnight Saturday and was not broken until after nine or ten o'clock mass on Sunday. Churchgoers had really worked up an appetite by the end of the service. Yet another theory is that brunch was started in New York in the many restaurants serving everything from lox and bagels to eggs Benedict.

What we do know is that the first time the word "brunch" appears in print was in an article titled "Brunch, a Plea" by British writer Guy Berringer in *Hunter's Weekly* in 1895. Mr. Berringer suggests that Sunday should be celebrated with "brunch," which he describes as a "corruption of breakfast and lunch" that "combines the tea or coffee, marmalade and kindred features of the former institution with the more solid attributes of the latter. It begins between twelve and half-past and consists in the main of fish and one or two meat courses." Mr. Berringer really sells the brunch experience in his article: "The arguments in favour of Brunch are incontestable. In the first place it renders early rising not only unnecessary but ridiculous." Hard to argue against that. Mr. Berringer envisions a convivial, festive meal as he explains his vision: "To begin with, Brunch is a hospitable meal; breakfast is not. Eggs and bacon are adapted to solitude; they are consoling, but not exhilarating. They do not stimulate conversation. Brunch, on the contrary, is cheerful, sociable, and inciting. It is talk-compelling. It puts you in a good temper; it makes you satisfied with yourself and your fellow-beings. It sweeps away the worries and cobwebs of the week." That was that: the word "brunch" entered the lexicon. The *Oxford English Dictionary* went a step further, declaring "the combination-meal, when nearer the usual breakfast hour is 'brunch,' and, when nearer luncheon is 'blunch.'" Thankfully, today nobody goes to blunch.

There are some who suggest that Hollywood movie stars traveling across the country by train in the 1930s brought the custom of having a meal that combines breakfast and lunch to our country then. Traditionally there was a stop in Chicago in the late morning. It did not take long for restaurants in Chicago to capitalize on this opportunity and to serve a meal that combined breakfast and lunch, a sound business decision when you think it would be likely that some stars slept through the first leg of the trip and would be looking for breakfast. On the other hand, some may have stayed awake and were ready for something closer to an evening meal. Either way, brunch filled the bill.

THE ORIGINS OF BRUNCH IN NEW ORLEANS

Although the movie star theory makes for a good story, New Orleanians know otherwise. In New Orleans the tradition of brunch started much earlier than the 1930s. We can thank Elizabeth Kettering Dutrey Begue for bringing the idea of combining breakfast and lunch into one hearty meal to New Orleans in the 1860s. Elizabeth's brother was a butcher. He woke early and, after a croissant and a cup of coffee, went to work. By late morning he was far too hungry for a simple meal. Elizabeth, who had opened a restaurant in the French Quarter with her husband Hippolyte Begue, started serving a "second breakfast" for the butchers and dock workers in the area at eleven every morning. It was the only meal served at Begue's, and by all accounts it was spectacular. The restaurant was soon discovered by tourists to the city, especially during the 1884 World's Fair, and by the late 1880s a second breakfast at Begue's was a must on any visit to New Orleans. The quality of food at

Begue's second breakfast was so renowned that Madam Begue is considered to be one of the first New Orleans celebrity chefs. She wrote a cookbook in 1900 titled *Madame Begue's Recipes of Old New Orleans Creole Cookery.* Begue's is in the past, but Mme Begue's legacy lives on. Tujague's,

The kitchen at Begue's Restaurant [The Historic New Orleans Collection, Acc. No. 1974.25.29.24]

Opposite: Begue's Restaurant, c. 1909–1919 [The Historic New Orleans Collection, Acc. No. 1987.144.120]

a rival restaurant also serving second breakfast, moved into Begue's location on Decatur Street near the French Market after her death and is among the many fine New Orleans restaurants that serve second breakfast, now commonly known as brunch.

Sign for Tujague's Restaurant, c. 1949–1958 (The Historic New Orleans Collection, Gift of Mark Latter, Acc. No. 2015.0392.2)

JAZZ BRUNCH

On a weekend or a holiday, especially Easter Sunday or Christmas, a jazz brunch buffet that lasts for hours may be in order. Of course, at these brunches there are more beverages on offer than coffee or tea. After all, something always needs celebrating at brunch. It's somebody's birthday or graduation. It's a wedding shower or an anniversary. It stopped raining. The humidity dipped below soggy. Libations are in order! There are the perennial staples such as a mimosa and a Bloody Mary, but another brunch favorite here is the brandy milk punch. After all, what says morning better than a glass of milk? And what says festive morning better than a delicious boozy milk concoction?

The wonderful thing about brunch is that it combines two meals, so you can go early or sleep in and show up at noon. Brunches can be like any other fine dining experience with a menu of mouthwatering choices covering both breakfast and lunch items, or it can be a buffet. Both are good, but the buffet allows you to see all the offerings and devise a plan of attack. You can start with breakfast—some

Dick and Ella Brennan in the courtyard of Commander's Palace [Photograph by Michael P. Smith, Copyright © The Historic New Orleans Collection, Acc. No. 2007.0103.1.1.503]

egg dish with meat or seafood or French toast, pancakes, and sweet rolls. Then it's on to lunch: maybe some meat and a side of jambalaya or roast beef and potatoes. No, wait, there are so many seafood dishes to try. How will you ever decide what to put on your plate? Aah, what a nice problem to have. Perhaps a break between breakfast foods and lunch foods is the perfect time for another brandy milk punch.

Brunch is usually more festive than either breakfast or lunch. A jazz brunch at many New Orleans restaurants involves the participation of the entire dining room. A brass band wanders through the room playing jazz and encouraging diners to stand up and dance. After a brandy milk punch, it just seems right to get up out of your chair and form a second line with fellow diners to celebrate. A second line is a New Orleans celebratory dance that anyone can do. It only involves moving your feet, swaying to the music, and waving something over your head, usually an umbrella or, if you are at brunch, a napkin. No judgment and no lessons required to become an expert—just find your bliss and dance! These jazz brunches usually last for hours and necessitate a nap when you get home. They are a great way to spend the day.

We can thank Ella Brennan and her brother Dick for the concept of a jazz brunch. The Brennans are the first family of New Orleans chefs, and Ella headed up Commander's Palace restaurant. As Ella tells it, Dick called her up late one night in the 1970s while he was in London. From his vantage point in the lobby of the hotel, he saw one room where diners were eating breakfast in silence. Across the lobby there was a Dixieland jazz band playing, and the idea to combine the two hit him. He called Ella and said, "Ella, listen to this! Jazz brunch!" The rest is history.

RÉVEILLON

Another morning tradition is the holiday season celebration in New Orleans known as *réveillon* (REV-ee-on). Réveillon is derived from the word *réveil,* meaning "waking" in French. Today réveillon is celebrated more often at lunch or dinner than breakfast, but that is a modern trend.

It started out as a breakfast custom, not a dinner custom. In the nineteenth century the citizens of New Orleans were mostly Catholic. An important religious practice among these New Orleanians was to spend the first hours of Christmas morning celebrating the birth of Christ in a mass at St. Louis Cathedral.

Accordingly, attendance at midnight mass on Christmas Eve was a widely practiced tradition. Fasting before mass was required at that time, so by the time the family returned home at about two in the morning everyone was very hungry. A large feast was set out that included all the members of the family. The French traditional drink at réveillon was wine, but now that réveillon is celebrated at any time of the day, your drink choices are limitless.

Brandy milk punch has become a popular beverage to order on any occasion: no fancy attire or holiday required. However, it is traditionally a festive holiday treat, the kind served in your grandmother's cut-crystal punch bowl (the one you're hoping she leaves you in her will because you're her favorite grandchild, even though she won't admit it to her other grandkids). Should you find yourself in New

Orleans at a Christmas open house, holiday high tea, or Réveillon dinner, do not pass up a brandy milk punch. It is sure to enhance your holiday experience.

WHERE TO GET YOUR BRUNCH PUNCH

When it is not the holiday season, you can still find brandy milk punch served in New Orleans, because most restaurants, whether casual or fine dining establishments, offer brunches. Commander's Palace, located in the Garden District, is one of the most elegant restaurants in the city. Every meal is a festive event at Commander's, especially the Sunday jazz brunch, Ella's legacy. It is not a buffet, but the menu is extensive, and you are sure to find many tasty choices. Some favorite dishes are turtle soup, creole crawfish frittata, and cochon de lait eggs Benedict. The signature cocktail is the brandy milk punch. Commander's recipe calls for brandy, cream, simple syrup, pure vanilla extract, and freshly ground nutmeg for garnish.

Miss River restaurant in the Four Seasons Hotel has a milk punch that is made with banana rum, cognac, pecan orgeat (syrup), and milk. The appetizers on the brunch menu include a caviar service and duck and andouille gumbo. Entrees can be traditional like steak and eggs and shrimp and grits, or you can choose the more adventurous eggs crème de la crème with toasted brioche, creamed spinach hollandaise, and paddlefish caviar.

A more casual place for brunch that is a favorite with locals is Atchafalaya Restaurant in the Irish Channel. The wonderful thing about Atchafalaya is that they serve brunch every day they are open. No more Sunday scaries when you have a Monday brunch to look forward to! The menu includes huevos rancheros, duck hash, and crab cake Benedict. Of course, there is a milk punch on the cocktail list. The Atchafalaya version is a rum milk punch made with spiced rum, cream, nutmeg, allspice dram, and chicory.

Broussard's in the French Quarter is another fine dining restaurant that does a superb jazz brunch. With items like bronzed redfish, king creole pain perdue, and Josephine Benedict (a version of eggs Benedict that features crab meat and shrimp), it can be hard to decide what to eat. One of the featured cocktails on this menu is brandy milk punch. This punch is also on the menu for breakfast at Brennan's. Theirs is made with brandy, heavy cream, and vanilla beans, and it pairs well with their signature dish, eggs hussarde, a deliciously different take on eggs Benedict.

Of course, the French Quarter is home to other iconic restaurants including Antoine's, Arnaud's, and Galatoire's. Antoine's serves brunch most days and has a special jazz brunch on Sunday. Be sure to get the Oysters Rockefeller, a dish that was created here in 1899. Arnaud's serves Sunday brunch with some classic New Orleans favorites like grillades and grits, and chicken and andouille gumbo. Galatoire's makes a special milk punch made with bourbon and brandy.

For a delicious buffet-style brunch any day of the week, head to the Court of Two Sisters. This restaurant has a jazz band that plays seven days a week in its quintessential French Quarter courtyard. Items on the buffet include such classics as eggs Benedict. There are also a salad bar and a carving station. Desserts include bread pudding with whiskey sauce.

Dessert is a quintessential part of brunch. Some favorites are various flavors of parfait, pecan pie a la mode, and Louisiana strawberry shortcake. Special must-have desserts when you are in New Orleans include the white chocolate bread pudding at Dickie Brennan's Palace Café, the classic bananas foster at Brennan's, and crème brûlée at Commander's Palace.

If the English version of a clarified milk punch is your preference, try the Empire Bar at Broussard's for a traditional cocktail. Or go to Saffron Nola, an Indian restaurant on Magazine Street. Order the "Easy Money" cocktail, a clarified drink made with yogurt and tequila.

After indulging in the excellent dining experience of a brunch in the French Quarter or Garden District, a walk may be in order. If you are in the Garden District at Commander's Palace, wander through that neighborhood and admire the old mansions, visit Lafayette Cemetery, or shop on Magazine Street. If you are in the French Quarter, there is so much to explore: it is the oldest part of the city and the heart of New Orleans. Walking through the French Quarter is like walking through a living museum. If you dined in the Warehouse District, tour the art galleries along Julia Street.

On a beautiful fall Sunday, enjoy a brandy milk punch overlooking centuries-old oak trees in City Park on the gallery of Ralph's on the Park. Their brandy milk punch is made with cream, brandy, vanilla, and simple syrup. On the brunch menu are specialties like crawfish avocado toast and stuffed French toast. After brunch take some time to stroll through City Park, a 1,300-acre public park that is 50 percent larger than Central Park. It is just across the street. In the park you will find the New Orleans Museum of Art, the Botanical Gardens, and the Sydney and Walda Besthoff Sculpture Garden. Children will enjoy one of the country's oldest carousels (commonly known in New Orleans as the "flying horses"), Storyland, and the Louisiana Children's Museum. City Park also has the largest grove of live oak trees in the world, with some more than eight hundred years old.

We will probably never know who came up with the idea of brunch, but we can all agree that it was a great one. After all, is it really true that too much of a good thing is bad? Does anyone actually believe that? Clearly, putting two meals together like breakfast and lunch resulted in a new and wonderful meal greater than the sum of its parts. So, the next time you are listening to jazz at a huge buffet or just having eggs Benedict at your favorite neighborhood restaurant at noon, lift a brandy milk punch to the unknown founder of brunch!

CHAPTER FIVE

The Punch List

RECIPES AND VARIATIONS

The most sensible thing to do to people
you hate is to drink their brandy.
—ELIZABETH TAYLOR

Life is short and brandy milk punch recipes are endlessly adaptable, so don't hesitate to try these. With so many ways to create a brandy milk punch and myriad flavor combinations, there is a version of milk punch for everyone—and we do mean everyone. Vegan or lactose intolerant? You can still enjoy a delicious brandy milk punch by substituting canned coconut milk in any of these recipes. If you want your punch to be even more luscious and decadent, whip the coconut milk for two minutes. We include a sampling of recipes here, ranging from the New Orleans–style brandy milk punch and its close relative, bourbon milk punch, to the vastly different English or clarified milk punch recipes. Once you get the hang of making these, you can punch up these recipes with your own creative ingredients. (See what we did there?)

NEW ORLEANS–STYLE BRANDY MILK PUNCH RECIPES

A New Orleans–style brandy milk punch recipe calls for milk, brandy, a sweetening agent (sugar or simple syrup), and fresh nutmeg for garnish. Within those parameters are subtle variations that yield delectable cocktails. The recipes in this section explore the variations in ingredients. Try a few and see which ones you like best.

A note about bourbon milk punch: virtually any brandy

milk punch recipe can be made with bourbon. In fact, bourbon milk punches are readily available in bars and restaurants all over New Orleans. If you are typically a bourbon drinker, you may prefer a bourbon milk punch, but give the brandy version a try and enjoy the different flavor notes.

BASIC NEW ORLEANS BRANDY MILK PUNCH

2 ounces brandy
1 cup whole milk
1 teaspoon powdered sugar
3 ice cubes
Cracked ice
Freshly grated nutmeg

Add brandy, milk, and sugar to a cocktail shaker filled with ice. Shake for about one minute, until the mixture is frothy. Strain into a double old-fashioned glass filled with ice. Garnish with nutmeg and serve.

CLASSIC CREOLE BRANDY OR BOURBON MILK PUNCH

What makes this recipe unique is the use of homemade Cherry Bounce to replace simple syrup or sugar.

2 ounces brandy or bourbon

4 ounces half & half

1 ounce Cherry Bounce (recipe follows)

Dash of vanilla extract

Freshly grated nutmeg

Add brandy or bourbon, half & half, Cherry Bounce, and vanilla extract to a cocktail shaker filled with ice. Shake for about one minute, until the mixture is frothy. Strain into a double old-fashioned glass filled with ice. Garnish with nutmeg and serve.

CHERRY BOUNCE

Cherry bounce is a cherry-infused cordial that was a favorite of George and Martha Washington. It is often made with brandy (it was originally made in England), but it can also be made with bourbon. (This recipe calls for bourbon because that is how my grandmother made it.) Cherry Bounce is traditionally made in summer when cherries are ripe, then infused for months, and enjoyed during the holiday season.

3 quarts wild black cherries

3 pounds sugar

Bourbon

Wash and mash the cherries slightly but be careful not to crush the pits. Place cherries in a one-gallon container and fill with bourbon. Let it sit for a month. Shake the jar every other day. Strain off the liquid. Put sugar in a half-gallon pot and fill with water. Bring to a rolling boil. When it cools, add it to the cherry juice. To each half-gallon of juice, add a half-gallon of syrup. Bottle it up and use it in every cocktail that calls for simple syrup. It takes some effort to make Cherry Bounce, but the yield is so plentiful, you may only have to make it once, depending on your cocktail consumption. My grandmother made Cherry Bounce from cherries she grew in her backyard, but she served it on ice as a separate cocktail in summertime.

BRANDY MILK PUNCH COCKTAIL

2 ounces brandy

1 ounce rum

4 ounces milk

1 ounce simple syrup (1 part sugar and 1 part water, boiled until the sugar dissolves)

1 large egg white

½ teaspoon pure vanilla extract

Freshly grated nutmeg

Add brandy, rum, milk, simple syrup, egg white, and vanilla extract to a cocktail shaker filled with ice. Shake until all ingredients are combined. Note: the egg white requires longer and more vigorous shaking. Strain into an old-fashioned glass and garnish with nutmeg. This version is closer in taste and consistency to eggnog and is especially appealing as a holiday libation.

VALENTINE'S DAY MILK PUNCH

2 ounces brandy

4 ounces strawberry milk

1 ounce simple syrup

Freshly ground nutmeg

1 fresh strawberry

Impress your valentine with this cocktail to start off the morning. Add brandy, strawberry milk, and simple syrup to a cocktail shaker filled with ice. Shake for about one minute, until the mixture is frothy. Strain into a chilled old-fashioned glass. Rim the glass with nutmeg. Top off with a strawberry.

MARDI GRAS MORNING MILK PUNCH

Mardi Gras morning starts early. The Zulu Social Aid and Pleasure Club parade rolls at 8 a.m. You will need to be fortified well before that, so start your day with a morning milk punch and a large piece of king cake.

2 ounces brandy or bourbon
4 ounces half & half
1 ounce Cocktail & Sons King Cake Syrup*
Powdered sugar or whipped cream for garnish

Add brandy or bourbon, half & half, and king cake syrup to a cocktail shaker filled with ice. Shake that and your booty to get you in the mood for the day. Pour into a chilled glass or a plastic cup if you are walking to the parade. Top it off with a little powdered sugar or whipped cream.

*Recipe follows if you prefer to make your own.

KING CAKE SYRUP

If you want to make your own king cake syrup, here's a recipe from Emeril Lagasse:

1 cup granulated sugar

½ cup light brown sugar

1¼ cups water

1 cinnamon stick

1 vanilla bean, split and seeds scraped

Zest from 1 orange

In a small saucepan, combine all the ingredients and bring to a brisk simmer, stirring constantly. Remove from the heat, let cool, remove the cinnamon stick and vanilla bean, and transfer to a resealable container. Refrigerate for up to three weeks.

BRANDY NIGHTTIME MILK PUNCH

The wonderful thing about milk punch is that you can enjoy it in the morning at brunch or as you relax at the end of the day. This version is a lot more fun than a glass of warm milk.

2 ounces brandy or bourbon

4 ounces Clover Turmeric Ginger Milk

1 ounce Cocktail & Sons Oleo Saccharum Syrup

Dash of vanilla extract

Freshly grated nutmeg

1 star anise for garnish

Add brandy or bourbon, Clover Turmeric Ginger Milk, Oleo Saccharum Syrup, and vanilla extract to a cocktail shaker filled with ice. Shake until all ingredients are combined. Strain into a chilled old-fashioned glass. Garnish with nutmeg and a star anise.

You can purchase Oleo Saccharum Syrup on the Cocktail & Sons website. Oleo Saccharum is Latin for "oiled sugar" and is a common colonial punch base made by muddling citrus peels with sugar. Cocktails and Sons makes this syrup by combining orange and lemon peels with Louisiana sugar, topped off with fresh-cut lemongrass, toasted cardamom, and dried ginger.

MIDNIGHT DELIGHT

2 ounces Kohler dark chocolate brandy

4 ounces chocolate milk

2 tablespoons powdered sugar

Brandy-filled chocolate candy

This is *the* drink for chocolate lovers. If you can't get Kohler dark chocolate brandy, try making your own. Infuse 2 cups brandy with ½ cup of cocoa nibs, a vanilla bean, and 2 tablespoons chocolate simple syrup for 4 to 5 weeks, shaking occasionally. Strain and refrigerate.

Add dark chocolate brandy, chocolate milk, and powdered sugar to a cocktail shaker filled with ice. Shake until all ingredients are combined. Pour into a chilled glass. Drop in a piece of brandy-filled chocolate.

PLACES TO GET A BRANDY MILK PUNCH

Should you be fortunate enough to find yourself in New Orleans, here are some places to order a brandy milk punch. This list is far from exhaustive, so if you happen to be at another establishment and see one on the menu, give it a try!

BRENNAN'S BRANDY MILK PUNCH

Brennan's is the French Quarter restaurant where New Orleans milk punch got its start. Its elaborate breakfasts were fashioned after traditional creole feasts, which often began with an "eye-opener" like a brandy milk punch.

2 ounces brandy

4 ounces heavy cream

1 ounce simple syrup

¼ ounce vanilla extract

Freshly grated nutmeg for garnish

Chill an old-fashioned glass. In a cocktail shaker filled with ice, combine brandy, half & half, simple syrup, and vanilla extract; shake vigorously. Pour into glass and garnish with nutmeg.

Brennan's Restaurant

COMMANDER'S
PALACE
RESTAURANT
NOW
HIRING

COMMANDER'S PALACE BRANDY MILK PUNCH

Commander's Palace in the Garden District has been a New Orleans landmark since 1893. It is a world-class restaurant with leading-edge, haute creole cuisine that is not to be missed. Commander's Palace is also a traditional place for a lavish brunch.

2 ounces brandy
1 ounce simple syrup
½ teaspoon pure vanilla extract
1½ ounces cream or almond milk
Freshly grated nutmeg for garnish

Combine all ingredients in a cocktail shaker filled with ice. Shake vigorously, strain, and pour into a chilled glass. Garnish with nutmeg and serve immediately.

GALATOIRE'S BRANDY MILK PUNCH

Galatoire's is located on Bourbon Street. It was founded in 1905 by Jean Galatoire, who brought recipes and traditions from his small village of Pardies, France, to New Orleans. Galatoire's is New Orleans fine dining at its best.

2 ounces brandy or bourbon
5 ounces whole milk
½ teaspoon vanilla extract
1 teaspoon simple syrup
Fresh nutmeg

In a cocktail shaker filled with ice, combine the brandy or bourbon, milk, vanilla extract, and simple syrup. Shake vigorously. Strain into a highball glass filled with ice. Garnish with a light dusting of freshly grated nutmeg. Serve immediately.

Galatoire's
Galatoire's
33
BAR & STEAK

DICKIE BRENNAN'S
BOURBON HOUSE
SEAFOOD

BOURBON HOUSE'S FROZEN BOURBON MILK PUNCH

At Dickie Brennan's Bourbon House, the emphasis is on fresh, local seafood. The restaurant is also located on Bourbon Street and offers an award-winning frozen version of bourbon milk punch that is a must-taste. Theirs is made in a daiquiri machine, but a blender will work in a pinch.

MAKES 1–1½ QUARTS

4 cups vanilla ice cream
1 cup bourbon
½ teaspoon vanilla extract
1 teaspoon simple syrup
Freshly grated nutmeg

Combine all ingredients except nutmeg in a blender and blend for eight seconds, until slushy. Garnish with nutmeg and serve.

MR. B'S BISTRO'S FROZEN BRANDY MILK PUNCH

With its combination of warm Southern hospitality and classic Louisiana-inspired food, Mr. B's has become a French Quarter fixture since it was opened by Cindy Brennan in 1979. Although Mr. B's is known for its barbecued shrimp and gumbo ya-ya, its brandy milk punch also has a fan club. People have been known to hop out of their cars and run into the restaurant to grab one to go. Mr. B's makes theirs with house-made vanilla ice cream, but you can use store bought if you prefer.

2 cups vanilla ice cream
1½ ounces brandy
1 ounce milk
1 teaspoon vanilla
Nutmeg sprinkle as garnish

In a blender, combine all ingredients except nutmeg and process until smooth. Pour in a glass and garnish with nutmeg.

Mr. B's
BISTRO
Mr. B's
BISTRO

JEWEL OF THE SOUTH'S BRANDY MILK PUNCH

Jewel of the South is nestled on the edge of the French Quarter in an old creole cottage featuring a quintessential French Quarter courtyard. Its cocktail and food menus are inventive and creative yet steeped in history. The recipes showcase classic techniques with innovative, seasonal flavors. This recipe is from Chris Hannah, part owner and director of Jewel of the South's award-winning cocktail program.

1 ounce brandy or bourbon
½ ounce dark rum
1½ ounces heavy cream
½ ounce simple syrup
½ teaspoon grated nutmeg
¼ teaspoon vanilla

Shake all ingredients with cracked ice and pour everything into a glass with the same shaken ice. Grate fresh nutmeg on top.

ENGLISH MILK PUNCH RECIPES

An English milk punch is a labor of love. It takes time, patience, and a sense of adventure. (We're talking about milk curdles and cheesecloth, after all). However, the recipes in this section yield a plentiful portion of a fascinating libation sure to impress your family and friends.

MODERN ADAPTATION OF BENJAMIN FRANKLIN'S

ENGLISH MILK PUNCH RECIPE

6 cups (3 pints) brandy

11 lemons

2 cups lemon juice

4 cups (1 quart) spring water

1 freshly grated nutmeg

1⅛ cups (½ lb) sugar

3 cups whole milk

Zest 11 lemons, being sure to only get the zest and not the bitter white part under the rind. Squeeze 2 cups of lemon juice. Steep the lemon zest in the brandy for 24 hours and then strain. Add 4 cups of spring water, 1 freshly grated nutmeg, 2 cups of lemon juice, and 1⅛ cups of sugar to the brandy. Stir until the sugar dissolves. Bring 3 cups of whole milk to a boil. As soon as the milk boils, add it hot to the brandy mix and stir. The heat, lemon juice, and alcohol will begin to curdle the milk. Let the punch stand for 2 hours. Strain the punch through a jelly bag (or pillowcase) until clear. Serve cold.

Patience is an essential ingredient in an English milk punch, particularly when it comes to straining. Do not rush this part, because it is a key component and will have a measurable effect on the outcome of the punch.

Opposite: Straining curdled milk (AdobeStock/Maria)

KING CAKE CLARIFIED MILK PUNCH

This recipe was written by Ryan Wilkins of Bar Marilou. [We converted the metric measurements to imperial.] You can scale down the recipe for smaller groups.

SERVES 10–12

1 bottle Appleton Estate Signature Jamaica Rum (1½ pints)

6 ounces St. Elizabeth Allspice Dram

6 ounces Trader Vic's Macadamia Liqueur (Frangelico works as a substitute)

6½ ounces water

¾ ounce citric acid powder

1 bottle (4 ounces) El Guapo® Chicory Pecan Bitters

4½ ounces dark brown sugar

6 ounces whole-milk

edible gold leaf dust and king cake babies, for garnish

Mix all the ingredients *except* milk until the sugar is completely dissolved. Place milk in a separate container like a mixing bowl or large plastic container. Pour the cocktail mixture *slowly* into the milk. The milk will curdle: this is good. The slower you pour, the lower the pH. This yields bigger curds, which clarify more effectively and strain out more cleanly. Cover and let stand for one hour. Filter mixture through cheesecloth and again through coffee filters. You will need to change both cheesecloth and coffee filters several times to strain the whole mixture. Store refrigerated for up to a month.

You can purchase Chicory Pecan Bitters on El Guapo's website. Made with freshly roasted Congregation Coffee, the bitters have notes of coffee, chicory, pecan, and cinnamon. You may want to buy more than one bottle, because you can use these bitters with all your brown spirits and, of course, with your eggnogs and milk punches.

BROUSSARD'S ENGLISH MILK PUNCH

Although Broussard's Restaurant serves a traditional brandy milk punch at its jazz brunch, you can get an English version at the Empire Bar in the restaurant. This one marries the flavors of pineapple with green tea and cinnamon. This recipe was written by Paul Gustings of Broussard's.

1 cup brandy

1 cup white rum

⅓ cup Batavia Arrack

½ cup brewed green tea

2 cups boiling water

2 cups whole milk

1 cup plus 1 tablespoon sugar

Juice of 3 lemons, strained

Juice of 1 additional lemon

Zest of 1 lemon, peeled in strips, removing pith

3 whole cloves

10 coriander seeds

1 (3-inch) cinnamon stick

In a large nonreactive jar, combine lemon zest, juice of 3 lemons, sugar, pineapple, cloves, coriander, cinnamon, brandy, rum, arrack, green tea, and 2 cups boiling water. Stir until sugar dissolves. Cover and refrigerate for at least 6 hours or up to 2 weeks. (The longer the mixture steeps, the smoother and more nuanced the flavor becomes.)

In a medium pan, bring milk to a boil. Remove from heat and add lemon juice; stir until the curds and whey have separated. Carefully add to the pineapple mixture.

Strain mixture through a large-mesh sieve, discarding the solids. Then strain the mixture through a fine-mesh sieve and discard the solids. Again, strain the mixture through a fine-mesh sieve lined with a coffee filter or double layer of cheesecloth. Replace the lining as needed. Cover and refrigerate until the remaining sediment settles. Ladle or slowly pour mixture into a new clean jar, leaving the sediment behind and discarding it. Cover and refrigerate until cold. Serve in a Nick and Nora glass. (If you don't have a Nick and Nora glass, a coupe glass will do.)

TEATIME CLARIFIED MILK PUNCH

Is it teatime or cocktail time? With this recipe, it's both. Perfection.

8 Earl Grey tea bags (or your favorite tea)

1 cup brandy

4 ounces rum

2 ounces Allspice Dram

¼ cup sugar

2 ounces freshly squeezed lemon juice

1 cup whole milk

Bring 2¼ cups of water to a boil. Carefully pour the water over the tea bags and steep for 4 minutes. Remove the tea bags. Add ¼ cup sugar to the tea and stir until dissolved. Add the lemon juice, brandy, rum, and Allspice Dram. Allow the mixture to cool to room temperature (approximately 30 minutes). Now it is time to curdle the milk. Pour the milk into a pitcher first, and then pour the tea mixture on top of the milk. Don't mess with it! No stirring! Leave it for approximately 1 hour, and let it curdle on its own. Use the straining method outlined in the King Cake Clarified Milk Punch recipe, and chill to serve. You can store your teatime milk punch in a quart-sized container.

CEREAL MILK PUNCH

The varieties of milk punch cocktails are endless. One of the more seemingly bizarre concepts for a cocktail is cereal milk, but it makes a surprisingly tasty milk punch. This recipe is an easy, one-off milk punch that lets you try the cereal-milk cocktail craze without the commitment of curdling the milk. The beauty of this recipe is that you can use any of your kids' sugar cereal you have on hand, like Cap'n Crunch, Fruit Loops, or Fruity Pebbles. (Make sure to set a few pieces aside for garnish!)

CEREAL MILK:

3 cups sugary cereal

3 cups cold whole milk

¼ cup light brown sugar

¼ teaspoon salt

PUNCH:

1 ounce brandy

2 ounces cereal milk

¼ teaspoon vanilla extract

1 teaspoon simple syrup

FOR THE CEREAL MILK: Pour cereal into a bowl, and then add milk. Let it sit for at least 20 minutes at room temperature. Strain the mixture through a jelly bag or cheesecloth, collecting the milk and throwing away the cereal. Add brown sugar and salt to the milk mixture, whisk until fully dissolved. Store in a pitcher in the refrigerator for up to 1 week.

FOR THE PUNCH: Pour brandy, cereal milk, vanilla extract, and simple syrup into a cocktail shaker filled with ice. Shake vigorously until the mixture is frothy. Strain into an old-fashioned glass with ice. Garnish with a few pieces of cereal.

SOURCES

BOOKS

Armstrong, Louis. *Satchmo: My Life in New Orleans.* New York: Da Capo Press, 1986.

Begue, Elizabeth, and Poppy Tooker. *Mme. Bégué's Recipes of Old New Orleans Creole Cookery*. Rev. ed. Gretna, LA: Pelican Publishing, 2012.

DeMers, John. *The Vieux Carré.* Baton Rouge: LSU Press, 2023.

Epstein, Becky Sue. *Brandy: A Global History.* London: Reaktion Books, 2014.

Fitzmorris, Tom. *Tom Fitzmorris's Hungry Town: A Culinary History of New Orleans, the City Where Food Is Almost Everything.* New York: Stewart, Tabori and Chang, 2010.

Forsyth, Mark. *A Short History of Drunkenness: How, Why, Where, and When Humankind Has Gotten Merry from the Stone Age to the Present.* New York: Crown, 2018.

Jarrad, Kyle. *Cognac: The Seductive Saga of the World's Most Coveted Spirit.* New York: Trade Paper Press, 2005.

McNally, Tim. *The Sazerac.* Baton Rouge: LSU Press, 2020.

Strachan, Sue. *The Café Brûlot.* Baton Rouge: LSU Press, 2021.

Ternikar, Farha Bano. *Brunch: A History.* The Meals Series. Lanham, MD: Rowman & Littlefield, 2014.

Wondrich, David. *Punch: The Delights (and Dangers) of the Flowing Bowl.* New York: TarcherPerigee, 2010.

———. *Imbibe! From Absinthe Cocktail to Whiskey Smash, a Salute in Stories and Drinks to "Professor" Jerry Thomas, Pioneer of the American Bar.* Rev. ed. New York: TarcherPerigee, 2015.

ARTICLES, THESES, AND WEBSITES

Adams, Jenny. "Antoine Peychaud's New Orleans Legacy Lives on in a New Bar." *Garden & Gun,* July 30, 2021. https://gardenandgun.com/articles/antoine-peychauds-new-orleans-legacy-lives-on-in-a-new-bar/.

Campanella, Richard. "On the North Shore of Lake Pontchartrain, a New Orleans Dairy Belt Was Born." *New Orleans Advocate,* June 2, 2023. https://www.nola.com/news/northshore/richard-campanella-the-birth-of-new-orleans-dairy-belt/article_c20151fa-fb32-11ed-b73c-03240622b0a9.htm.

"The Earliest Alcoholic Beverage in the World." Penn Museum, n.d. Philadelphia. https://www.penn.museum/research/project.php?pid=12#:~:text=Chemical%20analyses%20recently%20confirmed%20that,in%20the%20 Yellow%20 River%20 Valley.

Greene, Aislyn. "6 Things to Know about New Orleans' Booze Culture." AFAR, January 23, 2024. https://www.afar.com/magazine/6-things-to-know-about-new-orleans-booze-culture.

Guly, Henry. "Medicinal Brandy." *Resuscitation* 82, no. 7.2 (2011): 951–54. https://www.ncbi.nlm.nih.gov/pmc/articles/PMC3117141/.

"History of Absinthe in New Orleans." Explore Louisiana, n.d. https://www.explorelouisiana.com/articles/history-absinthe-new-orleans.

"History of New Orleans Cocktails, from the Sazerac to the Hurricane Drink." New Orleans.com, n.d. https://www.neworleans.com/things-to-do/history/the-history-of-the-cocktail-and-new-orleans/.

Jarrett, Mindy M. "'Drinking' about the Past: Bar Culture in Antebellum New Orleans." Master's thesis, University of New Orleans, 2018. https://scholarworks.uno.edu/cgi/viewcontent.cgi?article=3685&context=td.

Krewe of Okeanos. https://kreweofokeanos.org/.

Magill, John. "'The Liquor Capital of America'—New Orleans during Prohibition." Historic New Orleans Collection, October 8, 2018. https://www.hnoc.org/publications/first-draft/liquor-capital-america%E2%80%94new-orleans-during-prohibition/.

Nespor, Cassie "Medicinal Alcohol and Prohibition." Melnick Medical Museum, April 7, 2010. https://melnickmedicalmuseum.com/2010/04/07/medicinal-alcohol-and-prohibition/.

Rhodes, Jessie. "The Birth of Brunch: Where Did This Meal Come from Anyway?" *Smithsonian Magazine,* May 6, 2011. https://www.smithsonianmag.com/arts-culture/the-birth-of-brunch-where-did-this-meal-come-from-anyway-164187758/.

Wei-Haas, Maya. "The Unlikely Medical History of Chocolate Syrup." *Smithsonian Magazine,* September 6, 2017. https://www.smithsonianmag.com/science-nature/unlikely-medical-history-chocolate-syrup-180964779/.

ICONIC NEW ORLEANS COCKTAILS

The Sazerac

The Café Brûlot

The Vieux Carré

The Absinthe Frappé

The French 75

The Roffignac

The Brandy Milk Punch